M000025693

BOOK

OF

LEVITATIONS

Book of Levitations by Jenny Sadre-Orafai & Anne Champion
Published by Trembling Pillow Press
New Orleans, LA
ISBN-13: 978-1-7323647-6-9
Copyright © 2019 Jenny Sadre-Orafai & Anne Champion

All Rights Reserved. No part of this book may be reproduced in any form without permission from the publisher with the exception of brief passages cited or for educational purposes. Reproduction for commercial use is prohibited except by permission of the author.

Typesetting and Design: Megan Burns
Cover Art: Laura Vela
Cover Design: Matthew Revert
Copyedit: Kia Alice Groom

NEW ORLEANS

BOOK OF LEVITATIONS

Jenny Sadre-Orafai & Anne Champion

TABLE OF CONTENTS

I.

II.

III.

I.

PREDICTIONS

Like boys, you too were born with power—
you just didn't know how to steal,

asking politely, your fingertips
under your friend's body, chanting

light as a feather, stiff as a board, waiting
for her to hover, searching the night

for hidden constellations. Once,
you dreamed the moon turned red

and split like a peach to nurture you.
Once, you asked a Ouija board

who would marry you and it said
yes. You visited an old woman with tea leaves

who envisioned a black hole
in your spirit. Your psychic pressed

tarot cards to the table and said
that all your men would be lions

or tigers. You took aura photos
and finally saw yourself as a prism of light

refracted. You need no meteorologist—
your head throbs whenever there's a storm.

SPELL FOR DAUGHTERS WITH NIGHTMARES

You are your fathers—dreams happen to you.
Your mothers are first to feel the ruptured

breathing. They swaddle raw amethyst
(spangled mountain), put you and your sleep

on top. Fathers, footnotes, would cancel it.
Don't let them handle that. This is the best

you can want, daughters. You'll keep your voice
strong and young for when you need it awake.

SPELL FOR CORSETS AND UNDERWIRE

You'll always overfill
what's made to hold you.

Women have edges both sharp
and pliant, curving

for cupped hands, swelling
for children, shrinking

for love. Pull the laces
as tight as you can, force

every exhale out of you
for good. If you believe

thin lengths of metal
cushioned by flimsy lace

will be the only things
to shape you, then they will.

CONVERSATIONS WITH INHERITED JEWELRY

Turned to rust, chipped, links lost.
You wear the person too, so here

is the salve. Say to the bracelet
hung with loud charms, *no,*

that's not my name. Have a cordial
talk. It won't flail onto a neighbor's

dining table at brunch. No rings,
flat sapphire, drowned in a sink.

RAZE AN ABANDONED HOUSE

Empty fruits now. No one told the grass,
the weeds, the trees to leave. The sprinkler

is dry, directionless. How to make shapes
in the yard again, feet coming to home?

Chandeliers so bored with their glints;
unappreciated, they're Vegas headdresses

now. They watch weddings on work
breaks, shaking their noisy bodies

to object. Still, they won't be back by
the end of this spell. You'll have light

but it won't be in necklaces, broken
chains tinkling in the dark.

SPELL SAID IN THE VALLEY

Girls try to save you
in their backyard,
the trampoline dusted
with leaves. They say
they know the end
is coming: you won't be
taken by your ankles
to the good place.

The dip in mountain
is a secret mouth.
The girls are rotten
molars. You aren't saved
by them or anyone. You
ask the valley to close
her lips up, swallow
the people to sleep.

TRANSFORMING MEAN GIRLS

Become a storm chaser, catch
one by its placid eye and hold it
to your ear, hear the roar

that entrapped them, listen carefully
to its grief-stricken howls.
It'll shock you, this cacophony,

sad symphony of a litter of kittens
before drowning. Put this natural disaster
to your lips and blow it like a conch shell,

let the debris disperse like grey moths,
be careful not to let it blow back
into your eyelids—it'll strike you blind.

SPELL FOR DESTRUCTIVE BEHAVIOR

The secret is this: there's no way to find the pain

      before it finds you. You can't keep a fire

for a pet or chain it to your ankle and drag

      it through your days. Worship idols

of wrecked women, but know that they can't hear

      your prayers and you can't hear their loneliness

with the abyss breathing so heavy on your neck.

TAROT DECK FOR RAVAGED MEMORIES

Your card is the Empress—she holds a knife for a scepter. She has skin under her nails and claw marks on her belly. There are no men in this deck, but every card throws a shadow on the table in the shape of something a man did to you once. When you overturn The Lovers card, crows peck at the bones of carrion. The Sun is the moon and The Moon is a heart hovering in space. The Hanged Woman bears an image of you as a child, but you know this card means something about your father. The Joker glows as a shifting constellation of dying stars; the first pattern you can trace says something about your future.

WHEN TO CALL FOR AN EXORCISM

If you have a dream and your heart
is a tied bundle of smoke.

If all your friends' skeletons start to illuminate,
their bodies like neon signs of cheap motels.

If you look at a map, and you're unsure
if your country is a pistol or a palm.

If all your ice stops melting, especially
those cubes rattling around in your head.

ROADKILL RESUSCITATION

This is only for animals who haven't been
scraped up by taxidermists. Armadillo armor
shines in every Texas sun. We risk leprosy,
we cradle them—so many curled babies.

The first question when they wake up:
was it deliberate? We have to answer yes.
They need to be taught to keep out. They roll
into themselves when we say it.

They straighten out when they're done being dead.

SPELL FOR A WIDOW

Hear how the wind mouths the names of the vanished. It never stops. No one answers it back. The widow's chair creaks through long dusks and unthinkable daylights. Turn over her wrists; her veins a map that lead through grief. The dusty jewelry box. The muted piano. The satchels of baby teeth. The chandelier candles. The flames. No iridescent illumination, just half-lit peripheries crowded with apparitions. There's no such thing as resurrection, only endurance.

SHOVELS THAT DIG GRAVES

Too wide for backyard gardens.
Shovels forget though. Memories,
caskets piled, impatient, gone,
levitated from the blade.

Another relief—shovels don't know
what's in a casket. Clouds of balloons.
Fish flipping in flat water. Cities of maple
keys. Silk flower forests. Mermaids.

SPELL FOR DEAD LOVERS

I don't want them to wake me in the night
with those lips kissed in a past life.
Once, I told my young lover

to never get me roses: they'll only wither
and die, scattering their brittle shells
on my floor, cracking under my toes

like the sound of teenage heartbreak. Now
I know: Don't give me bodies either—
they'll die too. One boy erased

himself like his name was merely chalk
on a board, but I still see it—so brutal,
the lessons of ghosts. Another struck

by four cars on a bike. Skin regenerates
every few years, so the selves we used
to touch had already departed.

What, then, is this sting? On the sidewalk,
a trail of dead petals again—I must
pick them up, before this becomes

my wedding march. I fill my bra
with them so they shower my lover's
naked body. If I smell like dead

flowers, he won't notice the scent of dead
names on my tongue. Were you hoping
for a spell that halts grief?

NEW GHOSTS

Disclaimer: they stay
gone, disappeared bodies,
bone in dirt closets.

Here's the lift—they'll know
it's you, so be light, lose
your shape, your weight.

Set on fire their bike or
comb or china or shotgun.
That's not who they are now.

Their messenger is the first
animal across their grave
who won't speak your language.

THE GONE, THE DISAPPEARED

Your faces are age imagined.
Someone's looking

at a profile, saying yes
it's you. We saw you take

a boat in black light.
We swing you

home in a net, a room
of jellyfish cushion you.

This spell isn't for you.

It's for families who keep
your pictures pinned

in sacred rooms, who
burn tall candles

at church, who roll
milagros at dinner tables.

PALM THIEF

You came for my hand, my line,
lower and upper Mars.

I had read it—the wide space there.

You came to shake him loose from
the fist of a wife (me), clutch up

whatever treasure. I let you
rustle the gold, the man—

a picture I've seen when I was you too.

SPELL WHEN THE UPSTAIRS NEIGHBORS FIGHT

Picture dishes that levitate,
resisting hardwood floors,

picture shards shimmying out
of skin, finding each other

and melting together like clay.
Use the sounds you heard

from their lovemaking as a chant,
picture that's not his fist in the wall,

picture that his fist never finds her face.
Pretend that the blood red moon

doesn't ever look like a face to you.

SPELL TO STOP HARASSMENT

When he tells you to *smile, baby,*
do it, but make sure it cocks like a gun.

Make wind chimes of kitchen knives
and hang them in every doorway.

Find your sachet of baby teeth,
bury them in your cervix, and wait

for them to take root.
When you have a shiny row

of vagina fangs, fling your legs
open like an umbrella in a thunderstorm.

CURSE FOR THE MEN WHO HURT WOMEN

Know that you can paint lipstick on your mouth,
        you can smile to muzzle your voice,
and it still won't turn him good.

His arms clasping your naked body noose
        every living cell. He casts his light
like a lasso, drops daylight at your feet and withdraws,

taking slivers of you every time. He'll always be adored—
        the cock, his trophy of birth.
You could be any mantle. Don't wait

until you're dead to cast this curse: place chokecherries
        under his pillow, snatch sheets
off his body and let the naked night chill him.

Leave lipstick stamps on every coffee mug and dust
        the carpet with cigarette ash.
Become his ghost before he makes you one.

If he hunts you, bathe in gasoline and threaten
        him with a match—if you must
set yourself on fire to escape, do it on your knees,

tell him sorry, sorry, sorry.

INTENDED FIRES

You caused this burn,
a harm with no control.

You want the shift most—
ember to ash.

This is a destruction
designed. We'd heap

saltwater if we hadn't
already palmed it.

Drop cloths then. We wrap
the weeping willow,

flowerboxes you built,
geraniums in wine barrels.

SPELL FOR DRAINED PUBLIC POOLS

This will keep alive any animal
living there. What a reverse of
fortune or happy or summer.

This will fill it up, lit sequins
again at night swimming—
the only way for it to ripple.

This won't bring living people
back. They've given up. Deflated
their floats, garbaged their suits.

This won't displace the drowned,
the dead attached. It's not wrong
to do. The water is a cover

they reach for and they reach for.

ORPHAN SPELL

We come from motherless mothers, fatherless
mothers. Held breaths underwater, waiting
for parents to levitate back. We can't tell them
we know how to say *abandoned*. It's not a word
around them. We coo at their knees. We say
we will never leave. We will never grow adult teeth.

SPELL FOR WORRY

You must cast it out—it's worse than demon possession
or haunted houses and harder to rid. A priest can't uncoil
its suffocating grip. Sage can't snuff its gasping.

Once you realize that what life can give you is worse
than you can imagine, it takes root like a tumor.
As a child, a friend returned from Mexico with pouches

of worry dolls. She gave you one, fingertip height, bits
of colorful yarn spun around wire—too small,
you thought, to carry the burden of all that paralyzed.

Still, before you placed her under your pillow,
you held her tiny mouth to the pain and tried
to confess, though your tongue broke off

like brittle chalk. You couldn't shape it
into anything but a question: *What should I do
with my mind?* A tiny voice whispered back:

*Keep replaying the way it broke
until you can watch yourself break
without a flinch, as muted as bone.*

SUPER BLOOD MOON ECLIPSE AFTER PSYCHIC READING

Everyone was looking at the moon that night
      as black ink crept over its surface
            & blotted it out, as if the moon

slid on darkness like black fishnets
      and stopped dazzling us
            with bareness, a reverse strip

tease or a hallucination.
      The psychic had moons
            & stars & suns & crystal balls

& polished stones & piles of rings
      up to her knuckles. Her bangles clanged
            a warning, metal on metal,

but she told me everything was fine.
      She failed to warn me how some things
            will vanish, swept away by shadow.

Her trinkets felt pregnant with desperation,
      weak magnets begging for magic,
            & I felt so gutted and hollowed out

the night he left,
      when the moon turned red
            and disappeared.

HOW TO MAKE A VOODOO DOLL

A power like this must be authentically
crafted—you scavenge all the materials
like a bird weaving its first nest.
Comb out strands of his hair
when his head's between your thighs.
Get on top of him and let his sweat
drench your sheets and cut swaths
of his scent. If he comes to you reeking
of Jim Beam and Camel Lights,
it won't work. It's best to get him
in the morning. You need his pores clogged
with the dirt of him and you,
not scrubbed out with spiced soap.
Pop a button off his shirt, steal
the change that spills from his pockets.
Every man leaves a trail of himself
in a woman's home like a snail—
gather all the evidence of him in your life
like a ghost hunter. Shapeshift
his relics into a miniature of your longing.
Stab it and nothing will happen.
A true voodoo priestess cradles
her enchantments. When he's gone
for good, you'll have your doll.

SPELL TO DELAY THE END OF TIME

Know that what causes one wound
cauterizes another. Don't avoid

cliff edges. Build your home
on loose rocks. Drive rusted

cars. Avoid hunger. Plant,
but don't be fooled

by sweet juices. Know that
protecting the body of a beloved

makes you a prison guard.
Feed stray cats. Burn

something you once loved.
Know that when you kiss

a lover's mouth you enter
the throat of a hurricane. Get drunk

on rooftops, tear the limbs
off the dolls you grew up with.

Know that your head won't always
hold a swarm of locusts, but

your ribcage will always confine
a devastating plague.

II.

SALTWATER SPELL

I wring an ocean out in a palm,
leave it salted, flat.

Walking against no wave,
no schools peck at my leg.

It would happen by all our hands
if we let it. Coral evacuated.

I tell dogs walking on the beach
to lick salt from my feet.

HOW TO BE A SHE WOLF

There's no ritual for this: it's only will,
an unlearning.
                    Take the scalpel
to your belly and free
            the beast you swallowed.

File your teeth back into blades.
                    Forget
the way they trained you to heel,
            beg, sit, stay—
                            Remember,
you were born howling
            with blood on your jowls.

FOG INHALATION

Fog is real but so are gone spirits
stuck in incisors while you levitate
off a trampoline with no audience.

In the valley, everyone's extinct.
One yawn and a sip of steam
escapes. Girls who made you feel

bad. Teachers who mispronounced
you. Boys who touched you when
you said stop. Take the chin

of the valley, open its mouth.
Back goes everyone in single file.
Fog can be dangerous but not any more

dangerous than those who've died
because they weren't good, because
they watched rivers drain and didn't say no.

FOR LOST ANIMALS (EXCEPT BIRDS)

We feel backtracks. If animals can swim,
we hollow out a path, fill it with water
(whatever's closest—stream, lake, bay, ocean).
Their bodies know paddle.

If they can't swim, we throw light in a pattern
to their release. Pilots try to make out words
from the light. Some of us have fun with them--
But I loved you in cursive.

SCORPION SPELL

I let my skin get so dry
it transformed into cracked
desert sand.
        There came a time
when I didn't need softness
any longer.
        Tell me,
when did my tongue
turn venom?

Don't be fooled—
this oil blackened
exoskeleton still glows fluorescent
        in darkness.

I never wanted the paralyzation,
        only the sting.

SPELL AT THE DOCK

Eventually there's water, fish,
bioluminescent plankton. Last:
a ferry to spill you back. Wild

horses stamp to waves or moon,
walk into abandoned houses,
ruined, washed ecru.

Spanish moss or hair hangs
moody. Docks are not for diving.
They're for moving a hand into bye.

WEATHERVANE

Every body bare will know,
will say yes. I am desert,

an open mouth yes.
An open hand yes.

Maybe a prairie. The neck
young and long yes.

Toes split by grass.
Rain rolls into, pools on

bodies. Breaching, we
remind the water:

don't take our weather,
don't use it against us.

JAPANESE ARRROWROOT

A landscape choked uncontrollable,
undesirable. The gulping of rock,

land, house, ridge, cliff. A pest.
We can only disappear you by

choking back. You are
tucked in at every corner,

suffocated and unchained,
tethered to a dog's dewclaw.

SPELL WITH A COYOTE

I wake to her howl—a mother
hearing the thunderclap of an infant.

She wails at a hangnail in the sky tonight.
Love has lost its root like tiny teeth,

and I'm waiting for the fang.
Even when all was blunted, I gnashed.

When I walk in the middle of the night,
I think someone is with me, I think

there's blood on my feet. No,
I'm alone, no, it's only the red, red earth.

FERAL STILL LIFE

Notice how the sun glares
in hysterics, how every pulse

is a narcotic, intoxicating
the earth. Listen

to stray cats, their siren wails,
how they ache to be mounted.

Watch a cheetah rip the gut
out of a zebra and promise

yourself that you will never be
a predator's feast.

IN CASE OF NATURAL DISASTER

We can't collapse a tornado tail, a springed toy, flat.
Fold it into itself. We can't make it go felt.

Our sandbag bodies won't stop up floods. Our hands,
wood boards, don't cover what shatters. No.

Here's *HELP* across a house razed. Your pets
carried safely out in our mouths. *911* in debris.

REPTILES, BROKEN

It's a tail or fang or rib. They don't have
tongues that tell language humans know
yet. We're trying.

Take a pillowcase, submerge it in hot
pomegranate water. Rest it on the animal,
what's broken.

It won't be instant. The silhouette of
the wound is there until a skin sheds
or tail breaks.

HOW TO RESURRECT A DISSECTED ANIMAL

Wash your hands in formaldehyde, unknot
owl pellets and interrogate the tiny bones:

Tell me who you were before.

Put the skeleton together and superglue
its joints—there's endless power

in anything that's been consumed.

Place it next to the preserved corpses,
the mutilated flesh, the exposed organs.

Tell every curious onlooker to close their eyes

or else. Ask the maimed to wake, instruct them
to start tending to their wounds with their tongues.

MOTHKEEPER

Moths can be dead people. They bring
their bodies, furry, twitchy, to you—

on sun breaks between cutting hair.
You wear them on your wrists. Train

them to be stand-in earrings. I can't teach
you how to talk to them just like you can't

teach me how to make hair into ocean.
Your bedroom lights flick on, the smoke

alarm blares when you've held too many,
when there's been too much sun. Wrap

your clothes up. You made them hungry
for what humans have, for what they had.

SPELL FOR DYING HOUSEPLANTS AND FLOWERS

What's more profane than silk
flowers? Maybe plastic animals.

For the lazy, superficial, fearful of death.
Take the dying to the always living—

string of pearls to string of pearls,
Queen Anne's lace to Queen Anne's lace.

What wilt, you'll say. What a best garden.
What a bouquet in the foyer.

SPELL FOR MACHINES

Men think they've tamed the wild
with their ploughs mauling dirt,

their gears keeping time
by the hushed cracks

of even handed ticks. They've invented
factories that churn pesticides,

mutate tomatoes until
they resist both God and drought.

Our skies choke on drags of smoke,
our polar ice caps liquefy—

they thought they could make
everything stay.

TRANSMIGRATION

Mother, may I say you were a sun
in a life where I didn't know you?

It's a feeling you get.

Dirt on my soles when you were born
wearing velvet shoes and rosaries.

It's time to come home, Mother.

We draw all suns down with our hands.
It's not for us to cast you up.

FOSSIL SPELL

Low tide washes up the world's
bleached languages on stones,

tiny tunnels siphoning
sand from water.

The patterns we leave
might remain useful, distilling

the past from the future.
I know my voice has always

been vapor. I hope the earth
makes a memento of my spine.

SPELL FOR YELLOW

Take plates, dishes, yellow buttons.
Dig. Bury them. Find the yellow.
These dinner settings. A pretty yellow

button, all the harm. Answer the door.
Carry the load. Fasten the door. Climb
up into night, up the very truth.

Belong to things lost. A door must last.
The door must be here. Murder coming
fast and all the gold. All the safe and sound.

MANDATORY DISSECTION

Replace animals who didn't choose
to lose their song. In their places are

the leaping green who had to watch
themselves croon (silk in pools)

and then fall into chemicals made
to keep water clean. Fetched from

buckets burping beside chlorine water,
splayed deaths in the summer.

The others have homes again and croaks
they keep away from poisoned water.

SPELL FOR THE HIVE

Somewhere, there's a queen
in there, buzzing the honeycombed
tiles to breed a sweetness
you can taste. Save her—
you only have one good sting
in you. Make sure it's worth death.

Watch how the men serve her,
flying in a brainless rapture,
sacrificing until they are mutilated,
erecting the holiest shrine
from their hollowed husks
nosediving to the ground.

SPELL FOR OLIVE TREES

If I believe in forgiveness, will my limbs
    turn crooked and mangled?

Will my joints twist into knots? Tell me,
    how can I reach my branched fingertips

to the sky and make an offering
    of myself to God? The tree waits

centuries for peace, such supreme
    patience, and men break off

her branches, crown heads
    of bloody warriors with her leafy

touch. They uproot her trunk
    and twist her torso around a blade.

Glaze me in thick oil, let me
    drizzle rich fragrances

in my wake. Give me the plump
    salted flesh without the pit.

WIND SPELL

Don't ever ask the wind to stop—
you need its sorcery.

Watch how plastic bags levitate
so that you think

trash is winged and pulsing.
Your hair inflates

into a parachute around your body,
as if you've flung

yourself off the edge of something
again, as if you're

just a girl on a trampoline, letting
the wild wind

stroke you into a frenzy. Let it touch,
slap, sting, let it

contort, siphon, tear. Like a girl,
you've got to give wind

its freedom—let it destroy what it will,
it'll rest when it's ready.

III.

SPELL WITH A WINDOW

Every window has shaman powers—
       it wants to reveal
what you can't yet reach.
       It's full of symbols:
chrysanthemums in the garden,
       bug guts
smeared on glass, fissures
       in the frame,
the dirt path—which are you?
       Will you
go downstairs and walk out?
       Will you
shatter the window?

SPELL FOR A GASH

Find the exit wound, trace your fingertip
around its edges, kneel to the red crown

of the carnal. Dip your finger in its ink
and paint your body, mark yourself

with symbols of ancient ancestors.
Hieroglyphics of pain. You don't know

anything about power until
you can turn yourself inside out.

FOR A BRUISE

Cut an eyed wild potato
in half.

No one will ask why
it's here. That's yours.

Color will stop up,
hold its breath,

deliver your first
body back.

This works on hard
kissing left

on young,
young necks.

SPELL FOR BAD KNEES

Running is the bone grinder.
Ruined, bones carry a trunk,

arms, hands, head. Walking
looks like curtsying. Down

stairs sideways. Bone broth
at every meal. Broth shakes

for dessert. Slap the knees
growing fast. Watch a daughter

run your bridge, warn, *this is from
your grandmother* to her soaked back.

SPELL FOR NEW HOMES

Sage, holy water, black salt—
stack these in corners, smear

them in new rooms. Tie down
letters and spoons (from people

you can't miss back)—they
levitate on full moons.

Tell all insides of cabinets
something good, bright.

Hang one plant in each room
to clean the air.

Don't let in guests with mud
on their shadows.

MERMAID SPELL

Your daughter will tell you she's a mermaid
and you won't disagree—every woman

is born into an ocean full of baits and hooks
and traps. Take her to river banks

and watch her braid water with her fingers.
You need her to transform mythical—

napping on coral and seducing lonely
sailors with her sexless body

only to drag them under and bind
them in seaweed. Tell her crushed pearls

make seductive blush, that garlands of sea flowers
will sprout from her hair. You need

her dreams so badly that sometimes you wake
with sea foam in your mouth.

SPELL FOR THE UNBORN

The air isn't winged. Instead,
drain every energy source
of its powers until
you're buoyant.

The last thing to hold
you with conviction
is the body you unfurled
in, a woman

you may not love,
but a sorceress nonetheless.
If you watch closely,
she'll teach you how

to make gossamer
ribbons of smoke
rise from your eyelids
for every threat you meet.

BAPTISM RITUAL

Remember, in the womb you were gilled
and you never forgot how to breathe

while drowning. You won't require
submergence. You'll only need

to cocoon yourself: blankets
or lace negligee or steam. Then,

close your eyes and polish away your nightmares
like tarnish on a brassy piece of jewelry.

Imagine your body rippling and crashing
a coast, howling in the language of seawater,

your hair, a shredded white flag of surrender,
war weary and ready to cling to whoever

will touch it. You're finned, gulping
the salted wind—you emboss wet sand

with all the purest shapes of the monsters
you've been and the seraphs you'll be.

SPELL FOR CROPS

Pull down the water.
Keep out the dying animals.

Ask the bees, blind, to heel.
Plants understand

touch. Brush their stalks
to sleep, a small girl's

recess hair. Tell the juke
joint owners to open

their doors. Pick one bud,
wear it in a shoe until

your field is strong and wild
and finally here.

SPELL FOR TRAVELERS

Say thank you to your host,
the land, the water too.

If you sneeze once before leaving
your house, you're stranded

without exception. You've forgotten
some thing or some one. Check

the stove. Eat part of a good trip
ticket, swallow champagne for help.

Say four times,
so what if I'm escaping so what.

IN THE EVENT OF MEETING YOUR DOPPELGÄNGER

You'll know—a gust of wind
will jolt through the ribcage, electricity
will go haywire. Get in a car with her
and drive through deserts, seek

retribution like you would from a priest—
confess without a screen blocking you.
She won't make you get on your knees
and recite a dozen Hail Marys.

She'll pick up each broken fragment
of your other life, place it next to hers,
This fits here, she'll say, unafraid
of sharp edges or a little blood.

Together, archeologists of prehistoric
secrets excavated from wombs, you'll create
a mosaic of something whole. Each thread
in the tapestry of shame unravels,

the shrouds vanish and you can finally
see her, you can finally see yourself.
Unafraid, accelerate the car towards
a switchblade sky. The air will split in two.

WHITTLING CLIFFS

Nature cut off. Dramatic
rock or a disobedient chin.

Important life moments come
here. Ends of lives, confessions,

hard dives spraying its ribs.
This spell wants to grind them

in a pepper mill—a pebble
a minnow bites clean.

The view is unspectacular
and no one can be dangerous.

SPELL FOR MIGRATING FLOCKS

Somehow, you've been driven out,
by weather or fist, by cycles
or revelations, by need.
Follow telephone poles as highways,
listen to the cacophony of people
vibrating through wires.
If you touch a broken one,
you'll feel all the world's want,
all those voices clamoring for love,
zap through your body.
Unlike you, we abandon each other—
how much we envy
your steady formation.

SPELL WITH MAPLE HELICOPTERS

Whirlybirds,   maple keys,   flying

                    seeds. They

                                   fall in a   vortex

              of breeze. Pluck

                          them from your sister's hair,
trace the veins of their   translucent

                                            papery skin,   hold

          your sister's palm   and feather
the lines   that map   her destiny.

              Expose   the fortune
                                   no one can deny you:
daughters—
          wings

                          regenerate

          everywhere you look.

SEX SPELL

To succeed at this, you must
      sacrifice something holy.
Before the ritual, balance
      a crystal between your legs
and undulate in bed until
      you forget your spine, until
you shed your skin
      like a serpent.
The sacrifice must come
      from your body.
Figure out what's inside you
      that you can live without.
If you survive the sex
      you want most, you've failed.

BODY SPELL

Resist making a list of its sags
and disappointments. Focus

on the way it burns, on all the garments
it sheds, how it bears itself

and others. The ways you kneel
your body will define you:

in prayer, in apology, in pleasure.
Know that men will stare

into your eyes like stained glass,
that lips can concoct lullibies

or nightmares. Every man that
cups the breasts of a wicked girl

will leave her feeling
fever ridden, holy.

GOLD SPELL

In tiny sockets of gravel, you'll discover
something worshipful.

Whatever you find, melt it down,
cast it into a shape

that will adorn you. Crown
or necklace.

Filling or watch. Hold it
to the mirror

and watch your selves
multiply.

SPELL FOR THE GIRLS WHO WANT SPELLS

They block their own visions, huddled on my doorstep
      strung out on blistering cravings and forgetting,
believing themselves half mangled

by a beast they can't see. I hold a mirror
      to their faces and ask them what curse
made them think such purity

could be polluted. They breathe fog
      over their faces and weep that it's not fire.
They'll kill anything for the potion, their tongues

will contort into any ancient language
      I can teach them to unlock the trap doors
of yearning. I write down their names,

place it in their palms, and tell them to repeat
      it nightly a thousand times, until reverence
pulls them into its undertow—how astonishing they are.

PRAISE SONG

Praise creating the collage,
its kaleidoscopic silhouettes,
panorama of hypnotic symbols.
Praise the wildflower meadow,
the cascades of technicolor tongues
nursing butterflies and bees.
Praise the cicadas' cries
that clang like sharpening knives.
Praise the soldiers that cradle
wounded children more maternally
than their weapons.
Praise the bugs that desire
to annul a bomb's deaths.
Praise the girl that learns sewing
to stitch herself back up.
Praise the teetering
of an imperfect body, aroused
by its thirst, diving
into the tide to conquer
wild waves with craving.
Praise all the things
that flourish without you.

BREAKING THE FAIRY TALE CURSE

Rip the limbs off of a princess doll,
carry them in a gun holster. Put her torso
in a clear plastic bag and call it her glass coffin.
Protect her from eyes, shield yourself
from kisses that might awaken something.
Don't burn her red shoes, and don't dance
in any shoes that you didn't make yourself.
Wear a red cape everywhere, cloak yourself
in its fleshy vaginal petals, forget
about wearing your heart inside out anymore.
In every myth, there's a good girl and a witch—
you already know which one is more real.

RECALLING A SPELL

Say it backwards
in a black salt bath.

Clap your hands,
clearing the lines,

the girdle of Venus.
You won't make

a spell for two weeks.
Penance. Last,

burn a dollhouse back
to ember. Swallow the ash.

ACKNOWLEDGMENTS

Thank you to the editors of the following publications in which these works or earlier versions of them appeared:

Amethyst Arsenic: "Spell to Delay the End of Time"

Bateau Literary Magazine: "Spell to Stop Harassment," "Fossil Spell," and "Body Spell"

Bellingham Review: "For a Bruise" and "Spell for the Girls Who Want Spells"

burntdistrict: "Spell with a Coyote"

The Cortland Review: "Spell for Machines" and "Spell for Crops"

Dressing Room Poetry Journal: "Conversations with Inherited Jewelry" and "Mermaid Spell"

Gargoyle, "Spell for a Hive," "The Gone, the Disappeared," and "Spell for Drained Public Pools"

Hotel Amerika: "Fog Inhalation"

The Louisville Review: "How to Resurrect a Dissected Animal"

Menacing Hedge: "Mandatory Dissection," "Roadkill Resuscitation," "Mothkeeper," "Spell for Worry," and "Spell for a Gash"

Muse/A: "Spell for Yellow"

The Pinch: "Predictions," "Praise Song," "Saltwater Spell," and "Japanese Arrowroot"

Queen Mob's Tea House: "Spell Said in the Valley," "Spell for Corsets and Underwire," "Raze an Abandoned House," and "Spell for Dead Lovers"

San Pedro River Review: "Baptism Ritual"

Tar River Poetry: "Wind Spell"

Thrush Poetry Journal: "Weathervane"

*"Weathervane" was nominated for a Pushcart Prize by *Thrush Poetry Journal*

Anne Champion is the author of *The Good Girl is Always a Ghost* (Black Lawrence Press, 2018), *She Saints & Holy Profanities* (Quarterly West, 2019), *Reluctant Mistress* (Gold Wake Press, 2013), *Book of Levitations* (Trembling Pillow Press, 2019), and *The Dark Length Home* (Noctuary Press, 2017). Her poems have appeared in *Verse Daily, Prairie Schooner, Salamander, Crab Orchard Review, Epiphany Magazine, The Pinch, The Greensboro Review, New South*, and elsewhere. She was a 2009 Academy of American Poet's Prize recipient, a Barbara Deming Memorial grant recipient, a 2015 Best of the Net winner, and a Pushcart Prize nominee. She's a Professor of English at Collin College.

Jenny Sadre-Orafai is the author of *Malak* and *Paper, Cotton, Leather.* Her poetry has appeared in *Cream City Review, Ninth Letter, The Cortland Review, Hotel Amerika, The Pinch, Crab Orchard Review*, and other journals. Her prose has appeared in *Los Angeles Review, The Rumpus, South Loop Review, Fourteen Hills,* and other journals. She is a co-founding editor of *Josephine Quarterly*, Professor of English at Kennesaw State University, and Executive Director of Georgia Writers Association.

Trembling Pillow Press

I of the Storm by Bill Lavender
Olympia Street by Michael Ford
Ethereal Avalanche by Gina Ferrara
Transfixion by Bill Lavender
Downtown by Lee Meitzen Grue
SONG OF PRAISE   Homage To John Coltrane by John Sinclair
DESERT JOURNAL by ruth weiss
Aesthesia Balderdash by Kim Vodicka
SUPER NATURAL by Tracey McTague
I LOVE THIS AMERICAN WAY OF LIFE by Brett Evans
loaded arc by Laura Goldstein
Want for Lion by Paige Taggart
Trick Rider by Jen Tynes
May Apple Deep by Michael Sikkema
Gossamer Lid by Andrew Brezna
simple constructs for the lizzies by Lisa Cattrone
FILL: A Collection by Kate Schapira and Erika Howsare
Red of Split Water a burial rite by Lisa Donovan

CUNTRY by Kristin Sanders
Kids of the Black Hole by Marty Cain
Feelings by Lauren Ireland
If You Love Error So Love Zero by Stephanie Anderson
The Boneyard, The Birth Manual, A Burial: Investigations into the Heartland by Julia Madsen
You've Got A Pretty Hellmouth by Michael Sikkema
HEAD by Christine Kanownik
marginal utility by Tracey McTague
Unorginal Danger by Dominique Salas
Book of Levitations by Jenny Sadre-Orafai and Anne Champion

Forthcoming Titles:

Book of Monk by John Sinclair

It's Not A Lonely World by Erin M. Bertram

The Wound is (Not) Real A Memoir by Marty Cain

Trembling Pillow Press

Bob Kaufman Book Prize

2012: *Of Love & Capital* by Christopher Rizzo (Bernadette Mayer, judge)

2013: *Psalms for Dogs and Sorcerers* by Jen Coleman (Dara Wier, judge)

2014: *Natural Subjets* by Divya Victor (Anselm Berrigan, judge)

2015: *there are boxes and there is wanting* by Tessa Micaela Landreau-Grasmuck (Laura Mullen, judge)

2016 *orogeny* by Irène Mathieu (Megan Kaminski, judge)

Please visit tremblingpillowpress.com for details on our new book prize in honor of poet Marthe Reed.

NEW ORLEANS